Diary of a

Mad Hatter

A walk down an amusing road

Norman Rivera Gonzalez

ISBN 978-0-9979813-1-5

Inquiries & Contact Information:

nrgwriting@gmail.com

Facebook: NRG Writing

Twitter: @nrgwriting

TABLE OF CONTENTS

Foreword

What can I say about a Mad Hatter? In the most literal sense, is a mad hatter an angry guy who sells hats? Or is it a person with zany ideas who happens to wear hats? Is it the crazy dude drinking tea with a talking rabbit? Is it all of the above, none or yes? Does any of this make sense...probably not...or maybe...who knows?

Diary of a Mad Hatter is the latest written work of a dear friend who wanted to give a peek into the daily musing of a Mad Hatter, if such a thing is possible. Or maybe you yourself, standing on the subway platform, looking around you at all the people just waiting. Ever wonder about them, their lives, what they do or think? Do they like peach schnapps? Do they ever wonder about how others are thinking or perceiving them? Do they stay up thinking about whether or not penguins have knees or why are there locks on 7-Eleven if its open 24/7?

If you're now wondering the same things or anything else off the beaten track randomly, welcome to our mad house. That's the point of this book, to just enjoy life and it's many interesting

quirky twists and turns. Enjoy!

Rose Rivera

ACKNOWLEDGEMENTS

Many thanks to all my friends and peers who saw something special in my writings.

The clear majority were hypnotized with my first published book "Darkness and Lightness".

They were pleasantly surprised that I could touch their souls and enchant their minds with my prose and poems.

I thank the below influential friends, family and colleagues that pushed me to follow my dream of writing professionally.

My mother, Palmira Gonzalez Nuncy for always being supportive of my endeavors.

My number one fan and great friend, Joseph Bonanno.

My goddaughter, Nilda Velez who couldn't be distracted from the outside world when reading my work.

My good friend Nelson Lopez for egging me on and consistently asked when this work would be published.

My friend and professional advisor, Rose Rivera, for not giving up on me and taking my phone calls late at night.

My audience who wanted more and more of my thoughts in writing.

To everyone, who read my initial written drafts and loved them.

To those that in their unique ways asked, "When will your new book be published for all to read?".

I send my love and sincere thank you to all above and to you, the reader.

Enjoy!

Introduction

Waking up at the in the wee hours of day, that is if we can call it day.

It is still dark out.

At this peculiar hour the Mad Hatter's mind is inundated with so many thoughts.

Oh, what a clever mind he has!

Secretly giggling at the thoughts running through the spirals of his mind.

Thoughts that appear out of the nether.

He's unable to decipher whether these thoughts are from the realms of reality or fantasy.

Insane or just a tad unbalanced?

Honestly, he doesn't care if it's either or, he just wants to write before the thoughts disappear into thin air.

As he writes, a contagious laugher fills the room.

His laughter is alluring with an ambiguous attitude whether his diary is applauded or not.

He applauds on his own, relishing the moment of madness during these insane hours.

Honestly, his innocence creeps in, yes, he wants his diary to be liked by all.

A standing ovation revealing what millions of others have in common yet are afraid to express.

A cup of fresh coffee in one hand and a lit cigarette on the other.

Caffeine and another stimulant, that peculiarly illuminates his mind to the joy of writing, which he shares with an audience he does not yet know.

Yes, he is a Mad Hatter indeed.

Join his journey, there is nothing to fear.

Accompany him on this journey is what he asks of you at this very moment.

Beware, it will be a roller coaster ride.

You will be delighted with his innermost thoughts expressed through writing.

His "secrets" for all to see.

Some are vivaciously vivid in color and others are shades of black and gray.

You will attempt to conclude, if these thoughts are of the Mad Hatter, or someone else's.

Enjoy, he states gleefully.

You will never be the same.

May the innate power of every written word in this collection of

poems and prose touch you in a special manner. Yes, this is my special

wish.

Confessions of This Mad Hatter

Yes, I wear this unique hat.

Figuratively and literally.

A flamboyant beautiful that conceals many secrets.

Imaginative.

Thoughts of insanity that only others can comprehend.

Well, not necessarily insanity, although others may believe so.

Thoughts and views through lens that a unique few can grasp.

Flowers-Thorns-Lightness-Darkness.........

Impressions of the mind that are unique to me.

Only me?

Quite certain that others have these imaginative thoughts that course through their minds.

Being flawless is perfectly fine.

Some will describe it as peculiar.

Strange.

Not strange as these thoughts are relatable to many in the world.

Like those that prefer tea over coffee.

Similar to people that prefer scrumptious apple pie to sticky delicious pecan pie.

Both taste good, just a taste bud desire for different tastes.

No craziness, just zany and unique.

Take a moment to thoughtfully contemplate.

Which mad hatter do you relate to?

Lucky Penny

It was a typical winter day in the month of January.

Taking my time to run errands and observe surroundings.

It snowed consistently, but not enough to stick to the ground.

A frigid and gray day, I ensured to dress appropriately to stay warm and carry my umbrella.

I looked with glee at the snow that covered the cars and tree branches.

Although not many welcome the cold air and white snow, I find it refreshing.

I made sure I bought the coffee filters to make the freshly brewed coffee I love and find comforting on a cold day.

Milk, delicious snacks, Kaiser Rolls and all I wanted for comfort food.

A light breakfast with fresh coffee, what a delight.

I digress.

Something caught my eye just before reentering my building.

There was a penny on the sidewalk, a few steps from arriving home.

It was wet and gleamed.

It appeared the penny wanted shelter from the snow and cold weather, seeking warmth.

The inner child in me found it alluring, inviting.

As silly as it may seem, I found that it felt alone and seeking shelter from the winter weather

Yes, others may consider this special penny an inanimate object, yet, it had this unique effect on me.

I contemplated for what seemed a minute, but it was only a few seconds.

I picked it up, adopted the penny and cheerfully put it safely in my coat pocket.

As unusual as the action may be, it was normal for me.

When I entered my home, I joyfully removed the penny from my pocket.

I washed it under cool running water in my bathroom sink and dried it.

I named it my "luck penny.".

I accommodated it in a place where I can see and treasure.

A reminder, to give comfort or shelter to those that find themselves alone.

My lucky penny it shall be, all mine to admire.

Not Fixable

You will feel better.

You will improve.

Statements that may be comforting, but not true.

Do not sugarcoat the foreseeable.

Do not lie to make another feel better.

The truth may be a bitter pill to swallow but must be said.

You have not improved.

You have not shown signs of improvement.

You are not fixable.

Not fixable, perhaps for now,

Perhaps never.

You have a condition that is not predictable.

Irreversible.

Its ok, to accept you are not fixable.

Live with what you have and make the best out of it.

You live life and continue, with the hope that perhaps you may be fixed.

No more lies.

At the present time, you are not fixable.

Accept that, it's not forced.

It is easier to acknowledge the truth of the present.

You are not fixable for now.

Perhaps in the future, but not now.

The New Year

New Year, I welcome you with my heart and open arms.

The blessing of peace.

The abundance of love.

The daily bread that will never cease.

The reconciliation of past errors.

New Year, I welcome you with my heart and opens arms.

The love of family and friends.

The rekindling of old friendships.

The new friendships to come into my path.

The beauty in all I see and perceive.

The glass half full.

The glass overflowing.

New Year, I welcome you with my heart and open arms.

My connection to God in all manifestations.

The continuation of compassion in my heart toward mankind.

The offering of warm smiles to friends, family and strangers.

The realization of all my goals.

The uplifting of health for my family, friends and myself.

The joy and bliss that reigns within my heart.

The recognition of the Divine within my very being.

New Year, I welcome you with my heart and open arms.

The most precious gift, the Gift of Life.

One more precious day, precious month and precious year of Life.

New Year you are welcome, and I wholeheartedly embrace you into my life.

Cherish

Cherish.

Cherish.

Cherish.

Lovingly cherish each second of every minute of every hour of every day.

Today we are here and tomorrow we may not.

Capture every smile and laughter of all loved ones as if it's a photograph.

Ensure to record those moments in your mind.

Those will be many of the fond memories that you will hold on to.

Take those opportunities in the present to be in the company of those you cherish.

Do not take the presence of your loved ones for granted,

for they may be the last time you see them.

Time is only borrowed.

Daily embrace the love expressed to you.

Remember to say "I love you" before you bid goodbye to that loved one.

Vanquish and forgive unpleasant moments.

Instead, relish and bathe in moments of joy.

Remember your loved one's smile and contagious laughter.

Their smile.

Their laughter.

In their absence, all that seems insignificant in the now, will be significant tomorrow.

Cherish those moments.

Hug those you care for as much as possible.

Express your inner motions of love to the beloved,

your friends and family.

No bars held.

Enjoy and relish every bite of every meal,

every sip of that savory wine.

Savor the dish before you.

Chew every bite of your meal as if it was the last one.

Your taste buds will love it.

Forgive those that may have inadvertently hurt you.

Ask forgiveness to those that you may have hurt.

Let go of pettiness and focus on the blessings you have.

Appreciate and embrace the blessings of friends and family.

Make it a point to reach out to loved ones as frequently as time allows.

Time is borrowed on this earthly plane.

Before saying goodbye to someone, say it with a loving smile.

Let that be recorded in your mind.

Look at the skies, sun, moon and stars with the wonderment of an innocent child.

Cherish all moments.

Cherish and remember.

Cherish.

Cherish.

Cherish.

Cherish.

Once you cherish all these beautiful moments, you will have nothing to regret,

only good memories to recall.

Love and be loved.

Extinguish all the trivial trespasses you have experienced.

They are momentary and not worth harboring in your mind or soul.

Remove all thorns from your heart.

Allow only love to inundate your very soul.

This, will bring you undeniable peace and happiness to your inner being.

Take a moment to call a friend or family member.

Take a moment of your time to see them face to face.

It can be five minutes, hours or days.

Catch up on your life experiences and shared memories.

Live life to the fullest degree today,

as we do not know what tomorrow brings.

Live every second as if it was your last.

Cherish.

Cherish.

Cherish.

Cherish.

La Virgen Milagrosa

On my way to pick up my new eyeglasses and late take out dinner, I decided to take a different route to my destination.

I wanted to see different tree lined streets and sites.

I took my time, I was not in a rush to reach my destinations.

As I walked down the street, I came across a statue standing in front of a house.

It caught my attention.

Initially, I did not recognize the statue, which made me curious to look closer.

I assume the statue was there for many years and eroded with time and weather.

It was a statue of the Virgen Mary in one of her apparitions as La Virgen Milagrosa.

I could see her bowed head and graceful stretched out arms.

I was in awe of this statue.

Although the image was eroded and possibly unrecognizable to many, I knew who she was.

The paint had peeled, and the cement material was chipped.

Yet, I was able to look beyond the imperfections and I found beauty in the religious statue.

I decided to stay a minute in front of Her image, greet her and make the sign of the cross.

The statue was still beautiful, flaws and all.

Yesterday in my kitchen, I was washing dishes and thinking of my beloved family member who is hospitalized.

As I thought of him, peripherally, I saw an image of La Virgen Milagrosa.

The image I saw gave me hope and comfort.

Coincidence?

Not to me, all is connected in a magnificent way.

Perhaps, tomorrow I'll visit her again.

Mending a Broken Heart

I made it a point to not sleep in a fetal position as to not fall into a deep sleep.

Waking up at the early hours of the morning was a necessity as to not miss my scheduled appointment.

Laying on my back, was just that.

It was more like, relaxing my mind.

Allowing my thoughts to wander, hoping that my visit to the hospital would mend my broken heart.

My friend graciously offered to accompany me to this special visit.

He also did not rest as to make it on time to pick me up and comfort me during this quest.

We laughed and reminisced about our longtime friendship.

Very fond memorable moments.

Who knew that all these years later, we would ride in his car to seek a remedy for my broken heart.

It was a dark, rainy morning when we arrived at our destination.

Arrived earlier than scheduled.

As we entered the brightly lit lobby of the building, we encountered painted smiling faces to greet us.

Undeniably, the staff was trained to welcome visitors and patients with a dental commercial smile.

Although the smiles appeared genuine, to the trained eye, it was forced.

I registered for my appointment by another young man, like a robot, with that similar smile.

He instructed us to take the elevators on the left where we would be welcomed.

We reached the eleventh floor.

Stepping out of the elevator, the floor was dark.

Most of the overhead lighting was off, we arrived early, and both medical and clerical staff had not arrived just yet.

As anxiety started to creep in, a staff member appeared, once again, adding a forced giggle.

All of the nurses, technicians and staff were friendly enough.

Similar smiles, masking their own personal issues which needed resolution.

Theatrics and very well played drama.

The medical staff, hiding the jadedness of their experiences in this chaotic sensitive environment.

Just another day for them, a new day for me.

Prepping me for analysis was an eternity.

I just wanted to mend my broken heart.

Alas, albeit late, the physicians arrived.

I was mentally prepared to undergo whatever was necessary to mend my broken heart.

I patiently watched every move as I was poked and prodded for the procedure.

My hope was that I would leave with a mended heart.

I was laid on a hospital cot to take me to the cardiac intervention unit.

Prepped once again in this icy surgery room.

My wrist and private areas which would be surgically invaded were shaved.

I insisted that the wrist be used for the procedure.

The wrist, believing it would be a speedier procedure.

No overnight hospital stays, so I thought.

The surgeon agreed.

A cold red medicated solution was applied to both areas to avoid infection.

It was not very comfortable.

I was lightly sedated intravenously.

It was a twilight sedation.

My mental state was groggy, sleeping and waking on and off during the procedure.

The procedure was painful, yet I did not peep a sound.

 I did not want to undergo any other interventions and possibly stay in the hospital longer than warranted.

The procedure did not take very long, yet the surgeon stated it was much more complicated than the previous one.

Shortly, thereafter, I was in the recovery room.

Famished, I was grateful that the staff brought over sandwiches and cookies to eat.

Monitored by nurses and a physician assistant,

they recommended I stay overnight due to the complications.

I was adamant and said no.

My desire was to leave the hospital as soon as possible and see my family.

My friend told me I was acting childlike and that I should stay.

I responded, "No.".

I slept due to the sedatives.

As soon as the Physician Assistant gave medical clearance, I hurriedly removed my hospital gown and proceeded to put on my clothes and shoes.

My friend and I impatiently waited for the elevators to leave the hospital.

He heated up the car as I waited in the hospital lobby.

Once the car was heated and ready to go, we were on our way home.

Grateful to have a friend like him.

I reached home and hugged my family.

My bed was so welcoming.

Yes, home, sweet home.

Peculiar Moment

Strange as it may seem, I experienced the most peculiar moment this morning.

When I woke up, it was a beautiful spring morning.

The sunrays were beaming through my window blinds.

As I started to make my bed, underneath one of my pillows, I found a piece of paper.

The paper was neatly removed from a white envelope, perhaps a piece of mail I received during the week.

Usually, I keep all mail I receive for a week before recycling.

I remove the bills I must pay and put them on my night table.

The rest I leave on my bed neatly piled to review.

Catalogues, unsolicited mail advertising services such as life insurance and credit card pre-approved applications.

I do enjoy looking through the clothes catalogues to see what's new for the upcoming season.

That paper, a corner from an opened piece of mail, made my mind ponder.

It was blank.

I couldn't determine the envelope from where this came.

My mind started to run its cycle of imagination.

Perhaps a bit romantically?

Love letters?

Did someone, leave this purposely under my pillow?

A written message in an envelope that was not complete and removed abruptly to not wake me up during the night?

If the latter was so true, how did that person get into my home without my knowledge?

Wouldn't it be romantic if the piece of paper was left by an admirer?

Yes, a silly imagination, wishing this was true.

Very likely, the truth is that the corner piece of paper originated from one of my opened envelopes and inadvertently left it on my bed before going to sleep.

Such a lively imagination.

I shall open myself to romanticism in real life.

Then, and perhaps only then, I may find a complete message sealed in an envelope.

Until then, good night.

New Day

It is September 28, 3:15 am, eastern standard time.

I have been awakened by the sudden departure of Mr. Sandman from my bedside.

No good byes, more like, until next time, as he caresses my eyes and mind.

I get up, brush my teeth and brew fresh coffee.

I shan't wonder why he left me so early in the morning, without a farewell.

Although it's still dark outside, it's a new day, new beginnings.

An early heard start to the adventures that await me.

Welcome, beautiful life.

Dressed in Black Tulle

I was enjoying a beautiful day at the park.

A sunny day with comfortable spring temperatures and caressing breezes.

The trees were in full bloom, with vivid colors of green.

Some trees bloomed with various colored flowers.

The parents playing soccer with their children, others slinging the flying frisbee back and forth.

People walking their dogs and playing with them.

I sat on the park bench, people watching.

Some folks running on the side pavement as part of their exercise regimen.

Some with ear phones, others not.

A beautiful day to indulge my senses fully capturing my surroundings.

Suddenly, the air in the atmosphere changed.

Menacing clouds appeared from afar.

Slowly, yet, dramatically changing the color of the sky from a beautiful blue hue to a dark gray.

The people started to scatter to find shelter from an upcoming dark, menacing storm.

I remained seated calmly as I watched all leave the park.

As strange as it may seem, a figure of a beautifully dressed lady was walking in the not too far distance.

Her dress attire was entirely black.

A black hat, covered in a brilliant black tulle.

It was evident the hat was made especially for her.

The tulle wrapped designed to loosely cover her face and neck.

Yes, it was a black tailored dress suit.

Black net stockings clung perfectly to her legs.

The jacket fit perfectly to her body.

The perfectly fit skirt was of a pencil design.

Polished black pointed heeled shoes.

Awkwardly enough, her presence did not fit this park environment.

As she walked closer in my direction, I remained seated in a frozen state.

My heart started beating rapidly and unable to move from my sitting position.

I smiled towards her as to not let her know of my growing sense of fear.

She stopped her elegant stroll directly in front of me.

Her greeting was kind enough yet felt terrorizing to me.

In return, I diplomatically greeted her, trying to mask the fear in my voice.

The lady in black extended her hand to introduce herself to me.

I returned the gesture and although her hand was gloved, I felt such a cold feeling emanating from her hand.

She smiled as I screamed in fear.

Out of thin air, we both disappeared to an unknown place.

Playful Muses

In the early hours of the morning, for some, late night, depending on your geographical location, I suddenly awaken.

The mischievous yet beautiful muses, have visited me once more.

Inundating the depths of my mind,

inspiring me to write my innermost thoughts.

These thoughts, very likely,

buried in the deepness of my subconscious mind,

Rising to the surface to share with you and all interested to read my words.

Oh muses, as tired as I may seem, I welcome your presence, your playful manner,

to entertain me and others as I write.

Certainly, a significance to share with all.

Although tired, I await your message.

Perhaps I'll understand your gleeful, curious language which you speak.

Until then, my muses, visit me once more.

Next time, kindly allow your communication to be clear and deciphered as to what you mean to purvey.

YOU ARE FABULOUS

Running to the bathroom with excitement,

elated to view himself in the mirror.

Straight out of an imagined Broadway musical,

He starts to sing "You are fabulous!", with chorus and all.

"You are fabulous with all that jazz!".

Manic.

Manic episode.

He doesn't care!

He is "fabulous!".

He looks at his image in the mirror with adoration.

Throws his arms upwardly in a dramatic fashion,

singing "You are fabulous with all that jazz!".

A smile from ear to ear.

He hears the imagined applause in the background.

Laughter emanates from the very depths of his being as he sings to himself,

"You are fabulous!".

Still smiling and laughing in the mirror,

inwardly he knows this is a peculiar display of affection towards himself.

He figures, who best to receive adoration and applause than from himself.

"...with all that jazz!".

"...with all that jazz!".

He is fabulous and with all that jazz.

Manic.

Uncontrollable display of mania.

"...with all that jazz.".

He waits for someone else to love him,

to adoringly and sincerely shout out accolades of his appearance and persona.

Until then, he will continue to display self-adoration in the privacy of his bathroom,

he will continue to love and praise himself in this peculiar manner.

"You are fabulous with all that jazz!".

Life Through Your Eyes and Ears

As you speak about your adventures in life,

my imagination goes into high gear.

As you share the photographs and videos,

I imagine myself there by your side.

By your side.

I live for the sights you have visited on your last vacation or trip.

I can feel the sunrays you described on your face and body.

I can feel and taste the moisture from the ocean spray that caressed you as you laid on the beach.

The relaxation of sitting by the warm watered pool,

I also tasted through your vivid description of

the scrumptious food and drinks served.

It delighted my palate as well.

How I wish I was wearing my bathing suit,

watching people enjoy the swimming and antics in the pool.

How I wish I could have enjoyed eating the exquisitely served food.

The cooling drinks under the shining sun with you.

Whether at the beach or by the pool,

At this time, I will relish your memories as if they are my very own.

Your enjoyment of going to the flashy and entertaining Broadway shows,

I live through your eyes and ears as you describe the thrill you felt by the sights and sounds of the musical play.

The memorable performances by the actors on stage and the accompaniment of the live music emanating from the orchestra just slightly seen below the stage.

Your visit to the beautiful botanical gardens hidden away from the lively city.

Your sight of the beautiful plants, the scent of blooming flowers and awe of majestic trees.

I see them, as if I was present with you.

My senses are on full alert.

The lively laughter at the new restaurant catering to a diverse and beautiful crowd of people.

The conversations you had with your friends and family at the eating venue.

The colorful seafood paella and sizzling garlic shrimp appetizers that was served and enjoyed by all.

The cool and fruity Sangria served in a crystal pitcher.

Through your senses, I imagine the delicious taste of it all.

Ah, I can't forget the entertaining conversations you overheard from others dining at tables nearby.

In all these scenarios, I am there, yet not physically.

I experience these moments of joy through your recounting these moments through your eyes and ears.

Perhaps one day soon, I can experience all you have shared once I feel safe to leave my safe haven.

Even if only for a few hours.

But now, I am imprisoned to the walls of my haven which is my home.

Imprisoned due to my state of my mind.

The short walks I do take within a three-block radius does bring some comfort, but not enough.

It allows me to experience the change of seasons.

The view of local home gardens.

A view from the outside of new neighborhood restaurants.

I take a quick peek to see the inside of the restaurants through their vast clear windows and quickly depart.

It has taken quite some time to leave the safety of my home for short periods of time.

I await the moment where I can meet and enjoy the company of my friends and family, Vis a Vis.

Perhaps soon.

Someday.

The Scissors

I was thinking about the scissors.

I search, and it took quite some time to find them, as if they were hidden from my view.

I wanted to groom my eyebrows.

I wanted to trim my sideburns.

I haven't made the time to go out and be pampered.

Perhaps, I didn't want to or felt I didn't deserve to be professionally pampered to look "good".

I found the scissors.

They are still in my sight.

I held them once in my hands and put them back down.

Not sure if I was deserving of self-indulgence.

They are grooming scissors used at hair salons by professionals to neatly and creatively make you look beautiful.

I haven't touched those scissors again.

There is something sinister about the scissors.

Is it really the scissors that are sinister or negative thoughts inundating my mind?

When I look at the scissors I think of the grooming.

Yet, I also look at my neck.

I look at my stomach.

Perhaps I'll put the scissors away in a safe place.

It's not my time yet.

Not just yet.

Perhaps never.

But the thoughts are still rummaging through my mind.

I ask the Universe to remove these thoughts out of my mind.

I have too much to do before I leave this earthly existence.

There are loved ones I must take care of and this must be my priority.

Once they are fine, then, I'll get back to these thoughts and contemplate.

The mind is so complex.

No Regrets

No regrets.

As I look back in to my past,

I have experienced life in so many ways.

Childhood was full of joy with hardworking parents.

All that they can afford, they gave me.

My mother a blessing, an angel in disguise.

I cherish my childhood friends from diverse backgrounds.

I did not see black or white, I saw friendship.

I still do.

I've been blessed with wonderful teachers and professors, both

academically and spiritually.

An array of colleagues within my career, many who have become long time sincere friends.

There have been times, where I've made unwise decisions and had to deal with the consequences.

Yes, those consequences rained upon my parade.

One lives and learns.

This is part of everyone's lives.

Do not be fooled.

There were very dark periods in my life.

Moments where I thought I would not survive.

Yet, here I am.

I was able to see a glimmer of light way beyond the tunnel of life.

That gave me the hope that those moments were temporary, and I would go on with the circle of life.

I am alive and well.

I have no regrets.

All past and present experiences were needed in my life.

No regrets.

My knowledge has shaped me to the person I am now.

I am ready to leap above obstacles and walk new paths, I have the tools from past experiences.

"Yes, to Life!"

Spring Soiree

Today is the much-anticipated party.

A get-together hosted by a good friend to celebrate life and the season of Spring.

My bright yellow and white gingham shirt beautifully pressed.

The white pants picked up from the dry cleaners yesterday, with a sharp crisp crease.

Shaving my face late last night, in order to have a closer shave this morning.

Grooming is not only a treat but a must for me.

Perhaps vanity, right?

We all have a sense of vanity in some way or another.

We all want to look our best, it is self-satisfying.

I look out my window and it's a perfect sunny Spring day.

It's early and I am still in my comfortable t shirt and lounge pants.

Time to brew fresh coffee and have a slice of toast with a spread of raspberry jam.

As I sip on the delicious coffee and take a bite from the toast, I start thinking about today's event.

An event I'm looking forward to attending.

Images in my mind of good friends I haven't seen in quite some time will be at this party.

Excited to see all of them and catch up with one another.

We will be joyously conversing over hors oeuvres and delicious champagne mimosas.

Once again, I look over the clothing I'm going to wear.

Perfect.

As I eat my toast, the telephone rings, or so I thought.

I ran over to pick up the call, but apparently, no one called, perhaps something I imagined.

The imagined sound of the phone ringing, reverberated within my mind.

I proceeded to prepare for the party.

I shaved carefully as to not nick my skin.

The warm water as I showered and shampooed my hair was so welcoming.

I used a special gentle facial scrub which leaves your skin so clean and smooth.

Exiting my bathroom with the towel wrapped around my waist, suddenly, unwelcome thoughts took over my mind.

I sat on my bed, still wrapped in my bath towel.

The thoughts became overwhelming.

Dark and dreadful.

Paralyzing, one may say.

As much as I wanted to go to the party, my mind was drowned with unbearable anxiety.

"Don't go to the party", my mind said.

Stay home and you will be fine, the thoughts will end gradually.

My mind said, "your comfortable home is your friend for today.".

I went back to where my shirt was hanging.

Such a beautiful shirt.

I put away the clothing I was about to wear, back to the closet.

Once again, dressed comfortably in a t shirt and lounge bottoms.

I closed shut the window blinds in my bedroom.

No light.

I laid in bed and wrapped myself in my bed sheets.

I convinced myself that there will be another opportunity to see my friends.

Sleep became my companion and inundated my mind and body.

We Are Not the Same

We may have many similarities in common, yet, we are not the same.

Our smiles and laughter are similar, yet, we are not the same.

Our sense of humor and our thoughts may be similar, yet we are not the same.

Our grieving may be similar, yet we are not the same.

The demons that we both battle, may be similar, but they are not the same.

Those demons may have similar names and characteristics, yet there are many levels to these horrifying creatures and are not the same.

Our brains may be similar in structure, but our minds are not the same.

Our minds process painful and traumatizing life events, yet we all react differently.

Therefore, we cannot assume how a unique individual reacts to these life events.

We cannot project what our reactions would be to another person's life events.

Our reactions are unique and although our intentions are good we offer advice or sympathy.

We cannot try to influence another person's emotions or reactions based on our own life experience.

Giving compassionate, constructive advice and offering help is all we can do.

We are not the same.

The Innocent Freckled Face Boy

I took advantage of this beautiful day to shop around my local stores.

It was a brisk cold day, yet refreshing.

Patronizing local businesses.

Arts and crafts, something that I like very much.

As I walked into the art store, I was shopping for nylon colorful ribbons, for a project I'm working on.

This store caters to all types of artists, including children.

Paints, brushes, toys, puzzles.

Puzzles.

While I looked at the vibrant colored ribbons looking for a specific width and length, I noticed a young mother and son.

They were a few feet from where I stood.

I overheard their conversation.

The young beautiful freckled face boy was about 5 years old and very well behaved.

Of all the toys in the store, there was one that caught his attention.

"Mommy, would you buy me this toy?".

The mother contemplated for a few seconds.

She responded, "This is too girly for you, let's find you a toy for boys".

When I heard her response from this stranger, I was aghast and caught off guard.

The innocence in his voice upon asking for the toy was joyful.

She proceeded to show him a toy for "boys".

He responded, "But, I like this toy, this is the one I like".

Articulate young boy.

He was adamant and politely insisted, he wanted the toy she referred to as "girly".

I did not want to intrude in the relationship between mother and son.

I couldn't help it.

I was puzzled.

I turned to look at her.

The look was one of sadness and disappointment.

Perhaps the look in my eyes and facial expression transmitted "my" disapproval of her behavior.

He is only a young boy.

Allow him to express his inner being.

I wanted to say something, but it was not my place, I was not the parent.

I looked and turned away.

Leaving the store, mentally I wished him well and blessings.

May his mother understand him some day.

Accept him as he is, an innocent young boy that wanted a special toy.

I continued my shopping spree, intuitively knowing, that the young boy will be ok.

Yes, he will be fine.

Not Within the Grasp of His Hands

In about ten minutes, dusk was about to turn to dawn.

With a keen mind and jumbled up tears in his eyes,

he realized that the abominable issues at hand would not get better.

The thought of leading a normal, "happy" life was no longer viable.

The world had a different plan for him.

The playing cards dealt in such an unpredictable fashion,

that he didn't know what daily life would be in store for him.

He thought he had all in control,

but the mighty energies of the stellar universe

made an inexplicable U-turn at the green light found at the crossroads of life,

a jolting somersault.

The world had a different plan for him.

Within a blink of an eye, he innately knew that happiness was not part of the plan.

Just the day before he was laughing and having a merry time,

but the universe rumbled and shook underneath his feet and had the last laugh.

Life is not fair, he thought with anger.

The world and universe gave no hint as to what was in store for him.

The inevitable was already present, but he was not ready to accept his destiny.

He blocked those thoughts and was in denial.

He saw that all he planned was falling apart before his eyes.

That man was able to inspire and help others, of which, fortunately he was grateful.

Yet, with all the inspiration within, he was unable to help himself.

Isn't that fucking funny?

A smack in the face?

Unknowingly, he was not destined to be happy.

He thought of those that stated that they were content with their current moment in life and would change the hands of time.

A damn lie.

 "Man up" he stated and prepare for a bumpy ride.

Yes, a rough ride ahead indeed.

The world is not for thin skinned people.

He said, "Unpleasantries are in store for all.

Yes, this will affect everyone, sooner or later".

Buckle up.

Wipe those tears and go forward.

Smarten up and expect the unexpected cruelties of what is ahead.

That is life, allow the dice to roll and deal with it.

In the interim, enjoy what little happiness you have.

Perhaps the man is crazy, so be it.

Don't fight the bitterness, it's a losing battle.

Allow what may be, be.

I Miss Our Conversations

Your transition was so unexpected.

Just a little over 2 weeks ago we were talking on the phone.

I'm being selfish, but, I wasn't ready.

I miss our conversations.

Our daily conversations.

I would call you or you would call me.

We would speak about anything and everything.

Our favorite TV shows, food, current news and political scandals.

I miss our conversations.

This might sound outlandish, but can I call you?

Is there a secret telephone number in heaven to reach you?

We never got to say goodbye.

Would you like to call me?

I promise not to look at the caller ID.

Let's have one more heart to heart conversation.

It'll be a lengthy one at that.

Perhaps, in my dreams you can call me or me, you?

Just one more conversation.

There will be some sort of closure, but, please know,

You will never be forgotten.

I miss you, my dear friend.

I await our conversation.

Goodnight and until then.

Wonder

As I walk daily through my neighborhood,

I am captivated by the tree lined streets.

My admiration of the trees is peculiar, full of wonder.

They seize my attention as I walk by them.

I am in awe of their presence during all seasons of the year.

These trees are majestic and strong.

Some small or tall in stature,

Nonetheless, beautiful to see.

The trunk, the bark, the branches, the leaves.

Some of the branches have a span of great length, others intertwined with one another.

Several trees bloom flowers admired by all.

Yes, beautiful and majestic.

During the summer, the green leaves glisten from the rays of the nourishing sun.

In the rain, they are also a beautiful sight, as the raindrops grasp on to the leaves and eventually drop to the ground.

During autumn, their leaves change color from green to shades that range from various hues of yellow, orange and red.

When winter arrives, the branches are bare, yet reflect strength, life and survival.

At times, the branches are heavy with snow or ice, sustaining force to continue their existence.

Beautiful.

I smile as I walk by these trees, displaying admiration and a greeting.

I wonder if they can sense my smile and admiration.

I wonder if they can hear my thoughts relating to their strength and beauty.

I wonder if they can hear my praise to the Divine and my murmured, yet sincere prayers.

Many of these trees have been around for decades or perhaps centuries.

I wonder what they have witnessed or heard as people passed by.

How are our thoughts, spoken words and actions processed by the trees as we walk by?

Do they laugh at our jokes?

Cry, when we cry.

Grieve when we grieve.

Rejoice when we are happy.

Do the trees transmit our thoughts, actions and emotions to the deep roots that sustain them?

It would be wonderful to have a conversation with at least one tree.

To listen attentively to the stories of what they have heard, witnessed and experienced.

Sweet Dreams

I'm very tired and sleepy.

Getting ready to bed.

Such a feeling of comfort as I laid my head on my pillow.

As my eyelids closed to sleep, I heard my name.

I was not very startled as this has not been the first time.

Recognizing the voice, I sat on my bed and heard my name being called.

I swiftly walked to the other bedroom.

Apparently, she was awake and needed me.

She was confused with the time of night and day.

My loved one couldn't recall if it was day or night.

She could not recall her last meal or if she had eaten at all.

I patiently explained the time of night and comforted her.

"Coffee, can I have some coffee?", she asked.

Something warm to soothe her.

No further questions were needed.

I went to the kitchen and brewed coffee with milk to make her comfortable.

I sat beside her bedside and chatted about the day as she drank coffee.

Once again, she asked similar questions and patiently I told her that it was night time.

As tired as I was, my responsibility was to make her feel comfortable.

We spoke some more as she started to recall her day.

Finally, she recognized the time and the meals throughout the day.

Once she was feeling comfortable and smiling,

I kissed her on the forehead and bade her goodnight.

Returning to my bed, a bit of anxiety overcame me.

This is only the beginning of sleepless nights.

I wiped the tears from my eyes.

Blessed I am as she will be with me, night and day.

The rest of these upcoming days will become easier.

I shall continue to see the glass half full.

I am not alone.

Sweet dreams, my loved one.

Times Square

She was onboard the #2 NYC train heading to an unknown destination.

Time Square station was alluring and got off, not exactly sure what she would find.

As she reached the top of the stairs and saw the streets, she was mesmerized.

Mesmerized by the sounds, the lights, and sights that surrounded her.

She was at the center of New York City.

The city that never sleeps.

Although daylight, the lights of theaters were burning to the maximum.

Broadway and Movie theaters.

Stores and boutiques of all types.

Newspaper stands.

Some selling antiques, clothes, and of course NYC souvenirs.

The street vendors busy selling souvenirs and clothing to native New Yorkers and tourists alike.

Hot dogs, big salted pretzels and chestnuts sold by vendors at designated places.

The sights seem all so familiar to her.

Her senses were overwhelmed by the chatter of passersby's.

The streets were crowded, and she decided to sit on a public bench.

She people watched.

Many folks dressed in the finest wear and others dressed casually yet chic.

It was very noticeable that some people walked in a fast-paced manner.

Those were rushing to buy lunch and return to their workplaces.

She was overjoyed yet confused as she couldn't recall how she arrived at Times Square at this very hour.

Very timidly, the young lady asked a lady where she was.

The response from the kind lady was, "You're in Time Square. Are you ok?"

She responded "Yes", but the lady knew she was not well.

The lady sat beside her to converse and make her feel comfortable.

Friendly chit chat.

A police officer was nearby, and the lady discreetly called him over.

The police officer was informed that the lady sitting on the bench was a bit disoriented.

He gently asked her questions and realized she was "lost" and apparently not of sound mind.

He told her he can help her find her way back home.

She told him, "I don't know where home is, where I live. I'm not sure how I arrived here".

She was lost.

Emergency medical help was summoned by the police officer.

The EMT's gently and professionally asked the young lady questions.

She responded with the same answers.

At this time, the young lady burst out in tears and asked for help.

She could not recall her name or her purpose in Time Square, her existence in life.

Such a sad day for her.

Such a sad day for a fellow human being.

She was taken to a local hospital and evaluated psychologically.

Her identification credentials were retrieved in the bag she carried over her shoulder.

No emergency contacts were found.

Her doctor's business card was in her wallet and he was immediately contacted.

The conversation was discreet.

The young lady was admitted to the nearby hospital until things could be sorted out and for psychiatric evaluation.

Eventually, the young lady will be released and will be fine.

Now, she clings to hope.

Hopefully she will remember her name and who she is.

Don't Overlook Your Blessings

We wake up early in the wee hours of the morning,

Brewing coffee or tea,

Brushing our teeth, running into the shower.

Quick breakfast with family and friends,

so that we can run out of our homes,

reach our destinations in an expeditious manner.

Accompanying our children to school,

so that they arrive on time and not late.

The daily grind.

Yet, many of us, forget to recognize the blessings in our life.

Many focus on the negative.

No one's life is perfect.

We have ups and downs in life.

If you reflect, you will notice you have more ups than downs.

Yes, many experience health, family and professional issues, its part of life.

Have you taken a moment to reflect on the Divine, in all his and her manifestations?

Have you taken the moment to thank the Divine?

The roof over your head, the daily bread you have consumed, even if just one meal?

Have you thanked the Divine, for the Gift of Life?

Waking up and acknowledge the oxygen in your lungs, another day of life?

Yes, we all go through trials in our life.

Life is not perfect.

Roses have virtues and visibly conceived faults.

The virtues of the rose, the beautiful scent experienced by your sense of smell.

The faults, the thorns that come along with the rose.

If we are careful, we can avoid being pricked by the thorns and just admire the beauty of that rose.

We can be pricked by that thorn, a lesson learned.

That slight wound of the prick reminds us that we are human and the bit of blood that oozes from our finger, reminds us that we are alive.

Be careful and focus on the beauty of the rose and try to avoid the thorn.

We all go through trials in life and many are unpleasant.

But if we take a deep look inside, the blessings outweigh the trials.

There is always a light at the end of the tunnel.

We may not initially see that light and may seem beyond our grasp,

Yet, that light is closer than you think.

If we did not have negative experiences, we would not appreciate the blessings of goodness, a blessed life.

It makes us appreciate Life even more.

I've certainly have gone through trials.

During times of desperation, I've lost sight of the light.

In due time, that light has been visible to me,

I see hope and the desire to live and enjoy life.

Whether good or bad times, I always give recognition to the Divine,

Giving thanks for all.

The Divine has been my rock.

I have faults and virtues, I am human.

I give thanks to the Divine for all experiences.

The lessons put in my path, so that I can learn and not repeat the same mistakes.

Appreciative for another day of Life.

A meal to have when I know others may not be as fortunate.

I give thanks to the Divine, for family members and close friends,

that have been supportive and stand by my side to help in my healing.

I pray for those that are going through difficult times which are greater than mine.

Do not praise the Divine only during good times.

Praise the Divine in all experiences of our life.

Now, we may not understand why we're going through a "low" in life.

Eventually we will.

If Life was perfect all the time, without challenges,

It would be a boring existence.

Enjoy life, through the good and bad events.

Have faith, there is a light.

Like the illumination that may be foggy at night emanating from a Lighthouse, but still present.

Don't overlook your blessings.

www.ingramcontent.com/pod-product-compliance
Lightning Source LLC
Chambersburg PA
CBHW041529090426
42738CB00035B/2